▶ Decoding Strategies

Decoding B1
Workbook

Siegfried Engelmann • Linda Meyer • Linda Carnine
• Wesley Becker • Julie Eisele • Gary Johnson

SRA
McGraw-Hill

Columbus, Ohio

A Division of The McGraw·Hill Companies

PHOTO CREDITS
Cover Photo: KS Studios

SRA/McGraw-Hill

*A Division of The **McGraw·Hill** Companies*

2002 Imprint
Copyright © 1999 by SRA/McGraw-Hill.

Send all inquiries to:
SRA/McGraw-Hill
8787 Orion Place
Columbus, OH 43240-4027

Printed in the United States of America.

ISBN 0-02-674781-2

7 8 9 POH 04 03 02 01

1 _____ _____ _____ _____ _____

_____ _____ _____ _____

2 Match the words.

seem   clip

meet   seem

clip   clap

clap   meet

3 Match the words and complete them.

teeth   ck

pick   an

that   tee

pan   at

4 (th) m a f t h n s i o a t h l t n h t r d p e t h h m r f t d o k c t h t h t e l f

(this) a t t a p t h i s d a d t h i f t h i s p a n a m t h i s s h e t h e t h i s h

5 Copy this sentence:
Keep the seeds in this sack.

_____

6 Find Part 6 of Lesson 1 in your Student Book.
Write the first word of these sentences:

5th sentence: _____

2nd sentence: _____

3rd sentence: _____

LESSON 2

1 _____ _____ _____ _____ _____

_____ _____ _____ _____

2 Match the words.

pit   clam

meet   meet

clam   pit

math   math

3 Match the words and complete them.

feed   ip

than   pa

pack   eed

clip   an

4 (th) l i f t h m s i a o t h l t n h t p d r e t h h l r i t d o c k t h t h p a t i h t

(math) i t h p a t h i s d m a t h m i t h i s p i h a m a t h i s s h e t m a t h a s t

5 Copy this sentence:

Fill that can and keep it.

_____

6 Find Part 6 of Lesson 2 in your Student Book.
Write the first word of these sentences:

3rd sentence: _____

2nd sentence: _____

6th sentence: _____

1 _____ _____ _____ _____

_____ _____ _____ _____

2 Match the words.

store   •   •   torn

rats   •   •   rams

torn   •   •   rats

rams   •   •   store

3 Match the words and complete them.

ship   •   •   or

math   •   •   ip

cash   •   •   ca

for   •   •   ma

4 (sh)   t h h s h w o s h e j w h s l s h o k h s s h t p w h t h s h l s h g h s h h

(for)   s h f r t f o r l h t s f o r u k w r o f o n f o r s h t l f o f o r m e i a m

5 Copy this sentence:
She can go with us.

_____

6 Find Part 8 of Lesson 3 in your Student Book.
Write the first word of these sentences:

6th sentence: _____

1st sentence: _____

2nd sentence: _____

1

_____ _____ _____ _____ _____

_____ _____ _____ _____ _____

2 Match the words.

gas • • milk

drink • • three

milk • • drink

three • • gas

3 Match the words and complete them.

last • • sh

sheet • • nk

sink • • ant

plant • • st

4 (sh) p t h s w a s h e j w h s l t h o k h s s h t p s h t h s h l s h t h s h h

(form) t h p r t f o r t h r s f o r m k w r o f o m f o r m h t l f o f o r m e f a t r

5 Copy this sentence:
Cats can drink milk.

_____

6 Find Part 8 of Lesson 4 in your Student Book.
Write the first word of these sentences:

1st sentence: _____

3rd sentence: _____

6th sentence: _____

1 _____ _____ _____ _____ _____

_____ _____ _____ _____

2 Match the words and complete them.

track • • ra

rash • • eets

creek • • eek

sheets • • tra

3 (ol) s r o l d f e a o l t h e l h u l o l e w a l f o l e e l m w o h s d o l l o t a w o

(do) t o g o f d o s e p o l d o o d h w r o t a l d o j a r o e d o l s k d o c o

(was) w a r s h w a s d p j l w e s s a w w a s k w a l t h o r w a s i w u s h w a s

4 Find Part 9 of Lesson 5 in your Student Book.
Write the first word of these sentences:

8th sentence: _____

4th sentence: _____

7th sentence: _____

5

1. What letter is on the cat? _____

2. What letter is in the pan? _____

3. What letter is in the truck? _____

6 Copy this sentence:
His clock did not run.

_____

LESSON 6

1
_____ _____ _____ _____ _____

_____ _____ _____ _____ _____

2 Match the words and complete them.

stuck • • eets

glass • • ock

clock • • gl

streets • • uck

3
(or) i r o l j p i a o r t h e h l u l o r e t a c k o r e a l m w o l s d o r r o r a o r

(was) h j w a s d p i l s a w w a s k w e s w a l t h o r w a s h w a s w u s h w s

(to) s o t o f t o s a t o l d o o t h e r o t a l t o k a d o e t o l p k t o d o f o r t a

4 Find Part 9 of Lesson 6 in your Student Book.
Write the first word of these sentences:

7th sentence: _____

5th sentence: _____

2nd sentence: _____

5
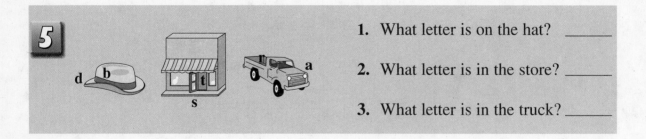

1. What letter is on the hat? _____

2. What letter is in the store? _____

3. What letter is in the truck? _____

6 Copy this sentence:
Can sheep sleep on rocks?

_____

1 _____ _____ _____ _____ _____

_____ _____ _____ _____

2 Match the words and complete them.

much •   • ich

chill •   • eel

which •   • mu

wheel •   • ill

3 Complete the words.

eep _____

eek _____

ra _____

ip _____

ma _____

4 Find Part 11 of Lesson 7 in your Student Book. Write the first word of these sentences:

1st sentence: _____

5th sentence: _____

3rd sentence: _____

5 (ee) e a o r e e s e i n g t h e o e e r p t l n e k f e e u m e u u o b d e e i n m

(to) m u t o t h e o n i s a i d t o t h e t h i s r a t o d l c h i p t o m a t t o

(said) i s t o a n o p a m s a i d r a s h s a d t h l s a i d w h e e s a i d t r i p s

6

S
u
f
l
f
b

1. What letter is in the glass? _____

2. What letter is on the horse? _____

3. What letter is on the bed? _____

7 Copy this sentence:
Show me how you do that trick.

1

_____ _____ _____ _____ _____

_____ _____ _____ _____ _____

2 Match the words and complete them.

which •   • op

chop •   • ees

trees •   • ip

slip •   • wh

3 Complete the words.

sh

br

cr

nd

eer

4 Find Part 11 of Lesson 8 in your Student Book. Write the first word of these sentences:

7th sentence: _____

5th sentence: _____

2nd sentence: _____

5

(wh) o l r s h s w h n g t h u l o r s h w h n e k f w h t h e u i t h w h e i t h o

(said) t o i s a n d s a d s a i d r a s h s a d t h e s a i d w h e r s a i d t r i p s

(she) m u t o s h e o n i s a i d t o s h e t h i s r a t o d l s h e p t o m a t t o m e

6 Copy this sentence:
Hand this bag of gold to that man.

_____

1 _____ _____ _____ _____ _____

_____ _____ _____ _____ _____

2 (wh) t h w s h h w h w r p l s n o w h t k h w h r e d y o u t h e r w h e e t l o f

(you) i n o n a t y o u t h i s p a n j y o u y a n o r e e t y o u l i s o f y o m y

(of) o n a f o r u n y p o o t h o f e a f o l t h o f o h h t a f o f i p g e o f r

3 Complete the words.

_____ eer

_____ eel

_____ wh

_____ eek

_____ wi

4 Find Part 7 of Lesson 9 in your Student Book. Write the first word of these sentences:

4th sentence: _____

2nd sentence: _____

6th sentence: _____

5

1. What letter is on the flag? _____

2. What letter is in the sack? _____

3. What letter is on the clock? _____

6 Match the words and complete them.

sweep • • ess

crash • • sw

think • • cra

dress • • ink

7 Copy this sentence:
Get rid of that wet sand.

_____

LESSON 10

1 _____ _____ _____ _____ _____

_____ _____ _____ _____ _____

2

(er) t h e e s h w h e r o r l s n o l h r e e r o r e r y o u t h e r w h e e t l o r

(of) o n o f o r u n j p o f t h i f o o f o l r h a f o r h j a f o f i u f e o f r t o p

(you) i n y o u o n a t t h i p a n j y a n y o u o r i e t e r s o f y o m y o u y a m

3 Complete the words.

_____ eer

_____ fast

_____ ow

_____ cr

_____ ock

4 Find Part 8 of Lesson 10 in your Student Book. Write the first word of these sentences:

7th sentence: _____

5th sentence: _____

2nd sentence: _____

5

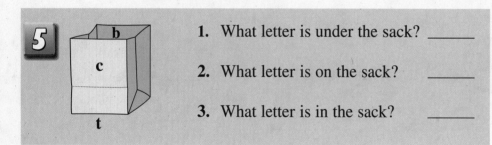

1. What letter is under the sack? _____

2. What letter is on the sack? _____

3. What letter is in the sack? _____

6 Match the words and complete them.

steep	•	•	bl
cash	•	•	ink
drink	•	•	st
blow	•	•	sh

7 Copy this sentence:
The snow was deep in the streets.

1 _____ _____ _____ _____

_____ _____ _____ _____

2 Complete the words.

_____ eep

_____ br

_____ ell

_____ dr

_____ m

3 Find Part 5 of Lesson 11 in your Student Book. Write the first word of these sentences:

1st sentence: _____

2nd sentence: _____

3rd sentence: _____

4

1. **Tim went down the path and got**

   to a c_____.
2. **The horse jumped.**
   Make an **H** to show where the horse landed.
   Make a **T** to show where Tim landed.

5 Match the words and complete them.

socks •   • ich

sweep •   • ocks

which •   • cra

crash •   • eep

6 (ch) c e r h c t h c h w h c h h t g l c k t p r s e e p o c h a t e r o c h c r a

(what) t a t h a t i s o f i n w h a t w e m u c h g e l c h w h a t i n o p l d e r h

(have) h a n d h a v e h w a t i s e v a h t h e n h a v e h e n h a t h a v e h o p e

7 Copy this sentence:
Tim asked a lot of questions.

_____

1 _____ _____ _____ _____ _____

_____ _____ _____ _____ _____

2 Complete the words.

_____ ck _____

_____ sh _____

_____ ck _____

_____ tr _____

_____ ore _____

3 Find Part 6 of Lesson 12 in your Student Book. Write the first word of these sentences:

1st sentence: _____

2nd sentence: _____

3rd sentence: _____

4

1. **Tim got the broom and began to**

   s_____.

2. Make an **X** to show where he got the broom. Make an **H** on the thing Tim's sister told Tim to lift.

5 Match the words and complete them.

_____ think _____ •   • _____ er _____

_____ mister _____ •   • _____ ve _____

_____ have _____ •   • _____ ink _____

_____ just _____ •   • _____ j _____

6 (or) h e u o n m r o i n g o r e r a p o r o j o m o r t e a l r m o r r e p r i s t

(how) w h o a r e o n w h o w h o t c k h o t i n h o h w e p j o n h o w s h o l h o

(one) o o f a n t a n o n i a p o n e n o o r i d t h o e o n e w h s h e o n e i r f s

7 Copy this sentence:
He told his sister what to do.

_____

1 _____ _____ _____ _____

_____ _____ _____ _____

2 Complete the words.

_____ br _____

_____ h _____

_____ een _____

_____ ing _____

_____ ders _____

3 Find Part 6 of Lesson 13 in your Student Book. Write the first word of these sentences:

1st sentence: _____

2nd sentence: _____

3rd sentence: _____

4

1. **Ron said to his mom, "I have no**

_____."

2. Write a **C** on the person who got a cop. Write an **S** on the person who put shells in the socks.

5 Match the words and complete them.

_____ said •   • ere _____

_____ after •   • s _____

_____ where •   • b _____

_____ back •   • er _____

6
(oo) o w e a o u o o p c k e o o s o o i o l d o o u t h s o j o o y o u e r o o i s

(are) e r a r a r e r o r a r e s l p r e a r e o f e a r a r e s t i n m e o u h j o

(my) y m y p c s d m e l y n y f u m y m j y o u i n o o m y t h a t o f m y b a c k

7 Copy this sentence:
You have lots and lots of socks.

LESSON 14

1 _____ _____ _____ _____ _____

_____ _____ _____ _____ _____

2 The words in the first column have endings.
Write the same words without endings in the second column.

stopping

robber   stop

hopped

3 Complete the words.

_____ unk

_____ g

_____ ill

_____ gl

_____ ck

4 Find Part 5 of Lesson 14 in your Student Book.
Write the first word of these sentences:

1st sentence: _____

2nd sentence: _____

3rd sentence: _____

5

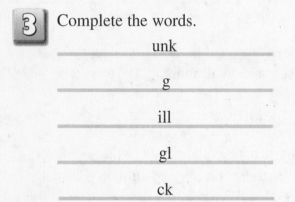

1. **The rat said, "I can help you _____."**

2. **He got a big chunk of ice in the bag.**
   Write an **I** where the rat dropped the ice.
   Make an **H** on the one who said, "I can
   hop no more."

6 (er) e r o r a r e i n o f m y w h o e r u s e r h o p t h r e i t e r s t o p w a s

(out) i n i f o f o u t o j l t a t o u h o u t y t o o l o u t g l a d t o o u t o l

(very) e v e r s t o p l i t t l e a v e r y s i t y o u v e r y c h u n k i v e r y e

7 Copy this sentence:
A little rat was sitting next to Kit.

1 _____ _____ _____

_____ _____ _____

2 The words in the first column have endings.
Write the same words without endings in the second column.

_____ clapped

_____ sitting

_____ planner

3 Complete the words.

_____ omp

_____ b

_____ ran

_____ ese

_____ pl

4 Find Part 6 of Lesson 15 in your Student Book.
Write the first word of these sentences:

1st sentence: _____

2nd sentence: _____

3rd sentence: _____

5

1. **Sandy went to the store and got ten packs of**

_____ .

2. Make an **X** on the one who eats too fast.
   Make a **P** on the one who has a plan.

6 (ea) a s w h o e a t o e s h e a s o e e p i n s h e r a t e a w h e a o a t s s h e

(some) s o s o m e f a s t s i t p l a n s o m e t h e n m e s o m e v e r y c h o m p

(who) h o w t h e n a t r a t e w h o r a n c h w h e n w h o d i d p l a n w h o a t

7 Copy this sentence:
Then she ate the oats at a very fast rate.

_____

LESSON 16

1 _____ _____ _____ _____

   _____ _____ _____ _____

2 The words in the first column have endings.
Write the same words without endings in the second column.

rider ————————•   •————————

hoping ————————•   ✕   •————————

shaped ————————•   •———— ride

3 Complete the words.

_____ own _____

_____ c _____

_____ aft _____

_____ wi _____

_____ ese _____

4 Find Part 5 of Lesson 16 in your Student Book.
Write the first word of these sentences:

1st sentence: _____

2nd sentence: _____

3rd sentence: _____

5

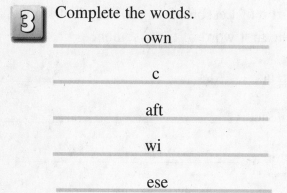

1. **Sandy had a plan to make the rat's rate go**

   _____ .

2. Make an **X** to show where the fast rat bit the fat rat.
   Make an **R** on the rat who said, "I made his rate go up."

6 (ing) l i n p e d g i i n g s r w i n g g j s r t n g e o i n g k v r u n g i t i n g

(some) s o n e r m e o n s o m e o l t m e s o m e p s e r s o m e i t o l d i s i n g

(lie) i e t l i e e r s a p c k l i d o o n e l i e i f i n n o l i e o r i n g l i p

7 Copy this sentence:
When this rat ate, it chomped slowly.

1

_____ _____ _____ _____

_____ _____ _____ _____

2 The words in the first column have endings.
Write the same words without endings in the second column.

saving _____

liked _____

maker _____

3 Complete the words.

oat _____

ell _____

tr _____

hamm _____

th _____

4 Find Part 5 of Lesson 17 in your Student Book.
Write the first word of these sentences:

1st sentence: _____

2nd sentence: _____

3rd sentence: _____

5

1. **The tramp went to the woman who ran the**

   _____.

2. Make a **C** above the person who fixed the lamp.
   Make an **X** to show where the tramp went to sleep.

6 (oa) a o r n o t o a a p o o u i o a s o a l f i n g o a o o u w h o a n e e d o a j

(come) c o r n c o m e i n c a m e p e t c m e o c o m e n o t o l d c o m e s o m e c

(work) w o n i f t h a t w o r d w o r k s o m a t c h w o r k w a n t e d w o r k i s

7 Copy this sentence:
A tramp went down a road.

LESSON 18

1 _____ _____ _____ _____

_____ _____ _____ _____

2 The words in the first column have endings.
Write the same words without endings in the second column.

timer • ———— •

rating • ⤬ •

hoped • ⤬ •

3 Complete the words.

____ ept

____ sh

____ hold

____ ea

____ eer

4 Find Part 5 of Lesson 18 in your Student Book.
Write the first word of these sentences:

1st sentence: _____

2nd sentence: _____

3rd sentence: _____

5

1. **The men and women did not cheer for the**

_____ .

2. Make an **X** on the person who tamped faster.
Make an **N** on the person who had to hold his nose.

6 (ck) c h w k t o c k k h c k t h i s g o c c e c k o l k c d e c k n o t h c h c k i

(your) y o p d y o u r r u n e c k j o g y o u i f y o u r s e e o u y o u r c h i n s

(answer) a n d s i t e a r a n s w e r n e e d l i p a n a n s w e r b i g n o t a r e a

7 Copy this sentence:
The men and women cheered.

1 _____ _____ _____ _____ _____

_____ _____ _____ _____ _____

2 The words in the first column have endings.
Write the same words without endings in the second column.

later _____

saved _____

liking _____

3 Complete the words.

oat _____

ch _____

boat _____

ean _____

b _____

4 Find Part 4 of Lesson 19 in your Student Book.
Write the first word of these sentences:

1st sentence: _____

2nd sentence: _____

3rd sentence: _____

5 Write the answers to these questions:

1. Another tramp came to camp. What did he look like? _____

2. Who was in the meet with Big Bob? _____

3. What happened to slow Bob down? _____

4. What did Bob do to keep on going? _____

_____

5. Who was the champ of the boating meet? _____

6 (ol) o l e r a l l o p o u a r o l t o s e e o a t o l i s e a e e l p o l i t e r s

(because) h e b e c a u s e t h a t n o b e s t b e c a u s e h o w t h a t b e c a u s e

7 Copy this sentence:
One day another tramp came to the camp.

1 _____ _____ _____ _____ _____

_____ _____ _____ _____ _____

2 The words in the first column have endings.
Write the same words without endings in the second column.

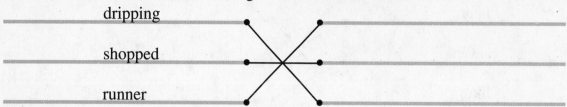

dripping

shopped

runner

3 Write the answers to these questions:

1. The tramp and his brother went to the shed. What kept them from getting in the shed?

_____

2. The camp woman got an old man to help. What did he say he fixed?

_____

3. What did Bob do to the lock? _____

4. What did the old man do to the lock? _____

_____

5. What did the old man think the lock was? _____

4 Match the words and complete them.

horn   sh

shed   br

pick   orn

broom   ck

5 Copy this sentence:
The lock fell from the door.

_____

1 _____ _____ _____ _____ _____

_____ _____ _____ _____ _____

2 The words in the first column have endings.
Write the same words without endings in the second column.

_____ rater •   • _____

_____ making •   • _____

_____ shaped •   • _____

3 Write the answers to these questions:

1. What did the con man have in his box? _____

2. Who did the camp woman ask to see how well the mop worked?

_____

3. How many mops did the camp woman take? _____

4. What did the camp woman give the con man? _____

5. What happened to the mops when they got wet? _____

_____

4 Match the words and complete them.

crack •   • gin

begin •   • m

moon •   • ad

glad •   • cr

5 Copy this sentence:
A con man came to the camp.

_____

LESSON 22

1 _____ _____ _____ _____

_____ _____ _____ _____

2 The words in the first column have endings.
Write the same words without endings in the second column.

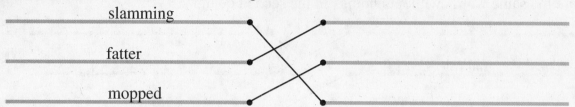

_____ slamming •   • _____

_____ fatter •   • _____

_____ mopped •   • _____

3 Write the answers to these questions:

1. Where did Cathy work? _____

2. What did Cathy and Pam go to hear? _____

3. Where did Pam lead Cathy to eat? _____

4. A man came up to Cathy and Pam. What was the man's job?

_____

5. How much did Cathy pay the man for the fish? _____

6. What did Cathy give the man in the fish shed to cook the fish?

_____

7. What did the man in the fish shed throw in for free? _____

4 Match the words and complete them.

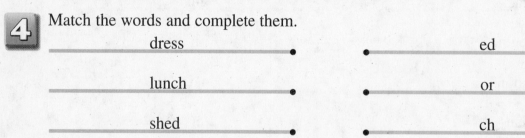

_____ dress •   • ed _____

_____ lunch •   • or _____

_____ shed •   • ch _____

_____ order •   • dr _____

5 Copy this sentence:
The shack was packed with folks.

_____

1 _____ _____ _____ _____ _____

_____ _____ _____ _____ _____

2 The words in the first column have endings.
Write the same words without endings in the second column.

_____ rider •⎯⎯⎯• _____

_____ timing •⎯⎯⎯• _____

_____ hoped •⎯⎯⎯• _____

3 Write the answers to these questions:

1. What was the name of Gretta's dog? _____

2. **Circle the answer.**

   When Gretta said she was going to the store, Chee

   • barked.

   • said, "Store, lots, of, for, no."

   • asked, "Can I go with you?"

3. What did Gretta help Chee do? _____

4. How big was Chee when she was one year old?

   _____

4 Match the words and complete them.

_____ back •   • th

_____ store •   • b

_____ helped •   • st

_____ things •   • ed

5 Copy this sentence:
Gretta left the dog at home.

_____

LESSON 24

1
_____ _____ _____ _____ _____

_____ _____ _____ _____ _____

2 The words in the first column have endings.
Write the same words without endings in the second column.

_____ bigger _____   •   • _____

_____ conned _____   •   • _____

_____ slopping _____   •   • _____

3 Write the answers to these questions:

1. The old clock maker met someone who was dressed up like a corn grower.

Who was that? _____

2. What did the con man get from the shed?

_____

3. Why did the con man get the big horn? _____

_____

4. What did the clock maker give the con man for the big horn?

_____

5. How did the con man feel after the trade? _____

4 Match the words and complete them.

_____ clock _____   •   • _____ rn

_____ corn _____   •   • _____ ing

_____ sled _____   •   • _____ cl

_____ conning _____   •   • _____ ed

5 Copy this sentence:
The con man liked conning folks.

_____

1 _____ _____ _____ _____

_____ _____ _____ _____

2 The words in the first column have endings.
Write the same words without endings in the second column.

_____ later _____

_____ saving _____

_____ liked _____

3 Write the answers to these questions:

1. Chee went to a fire station. What did she need? _____

2. Where did Chee go after she left the fire station?

_____

3. What did Chee need to do to get a job at the brick plant?

_____

4. Name 2 things Chee did after she did not lift the bricks.

_____

_____

4 Match the words and complete them.

_____ speak •   • ck _____

_____ brick •   • ch _____

_____ cheeks •   • ant _____

_____ plant •   • sp _____

5 Copy this sentence:
Chee went to a fire station.

_____

LESSON 26

1 _____ _____ _____ _____ _____

_____ _____ _____ _____ _____

2 The words in the first column have endings.
Write the same words without endings in the second column.

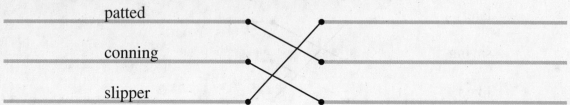

_____ patted _____   _____

_____ conning _____   _____

_____ slipper _____   _____

3 Write the answers to these questions:

1. What was the name of the rancher? _____

2. Name 2 things the rancher did well. _____

_____

3. Who had the biggest horse? _____

4. What was the name of the horse? _____

5. What did the rancher do every day?

_____

4 Match the words and complete them.

_____ slap _____   _____ be _____

_____ bent _____   _____ sw _____

_____ leave _____   _____ ap _____

_____ swim _____   _____ ve _____

5 Copy this sentence:
Each worker had a horse.

_____

1 _____ _____ _____ _____ _____

_____ _____ _____ _____ _____

2 The words in the first column have endings.
Write the same words without endings in the second column.

named

rider

making

3 Write the answers to these questions:

1. Where did Chee go for a job? _____

2. What did Chee do when she got mad?

_____

3. What did the woman show Chee how to do?

_____

4. What happened to Chee's rate as she worked at the job?

_____

5. How well did Chee stack slate after nearly a year of working at the plant? _____

_____

4 Match the words and complete them.

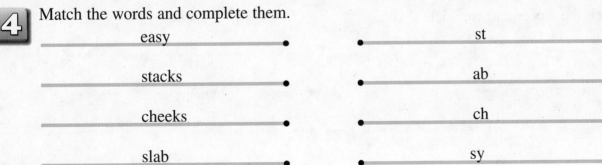

easy   st

stacks   ab

cheeks   ch

slab   sy

5 Copy this sentence:
Chee was not so mad now.

_____

1 _____ _____ _____ _____ _____
   _____ _____ _____ _____ _____

2 The words in the first column have endings.
   Write the same words without endings in the second column.

   _____ chopped •   • _____
   _____ dropping •   • _____
   _____ rubbing •   • _____

3 Write the answers to these questions:

   1. What did Emma send for? _____

   2. What did the con man tell the helper? _____

   _____

   3. What did the con man plan to do with the ten sacks? _____

   _____

   4. Name 2 things that the con man shaved when he was trying to shear sheep.

   _____

   5. Emma showed the con man how to do the job. What did she do to show him?

   _____

4 Match the words and complete them.

   _____ chest •   • _____ ch
   _____ steal •   • _____ eets
   _____ every •   • _____ ev
   _____ sheets •   • _____ l

5 Copy this sentence:
   The helper went down the road.

   _____

1 _____ _____ _____ _____ _____

_____ _____ _____ _____ _____

2 The words in the first column have endings.
Write the same words without endings in the second column.

shaved

hoping

timer

3 Write the answers to these questions:

1. The tramp had worked at the camp for nearly a year. Name 2 things he did there.

_____

2. What did the tramp plan to do after leaving the camp? _____

_____

3. What did the tramp do to show Emma that he was a fast worker?

_____

4. Emma made a deal with the tramp. What did the tramp have to do?

_____

4 Match the words and complete them.

melt   ing

bath   fl

flash   th

morning   me

5 Copy this sentence:
That made the tramp mad.

_____

1 _____ _____ _____ _____ _____

_____ _____ _____ _____ _____

2 The words in the first column have endings.
Write the same words without endings in the second column.

_____ sleeping _____

_____ nearly _____

_____ faster _____

3 Write the answers to these questions:

1. When the helper went to wake up the tramp, what did the tramp do?

_____

2. Where did the tramp and Emma go after he got up?

_____

3. Who went faster—the tramp or the helper? _____

4. What was the helper's job?

_____

5. Why did Emma drop the shears? _____

4 Match the words and complete them.

_____ shears • • ed _____

_____ beans • • sh _____

_____ sweeping • • b _____

_____ reached • • ing _____

5 Copy this sentence:
The shears flashed in the sun.

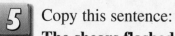

_____

1 _____ _____ _____ _____ _____

_____ _____ _____ _____ _____

2 The words in the first column have endings.
Write the same words without endings in the second column.

_____ grabbed _____●   ●_____ _____

_____ mopping _____●   ●_____ _____

_____ shipped _____●   ●_____ _____

3 Write the answers to these questions:

1. Name 3 things the tramp ate.

_____

2. Who said, "My tramp can beat anyone in a shearing meet?"

_____

3. Who said, "I think I can beat anyone in a shearing meet?"

_____

4. When was the meet going to be? _____

5. What did the tramp plan to do for the rest of the week? _____

4 Match the words and complete them.

_____ win _____●   ●_____ til _____

_____ horse _____●   ●_____ in _____

_____ until _____●   ●_____ be _____

_____ between _____●   ●_____ h _____

5 Copy this sentence:
Emma went to town and bragged.

_____

LESSON 32

1 _____ _____ _____ _____

_____ _____ _____ _____

2 The words in the first column have endings.
Write the same words without endings in the second column.

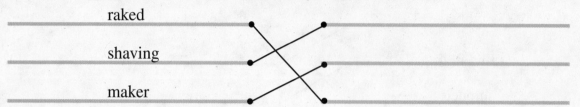

raked

shaving

maker

3 Write the answers to these questions:

1. What kind of shape was the tramp in at the end of the week?

_____

2. What kind of shape was Shelly in?

_____

3. What did the sheep do when the tramp ran the shears into the sheep's ear?

_____

4. How big was the pile of wool that Shelly had made at the end of the day?

_____

5. How big was the tramp's pile of wool at the end of the day?

_____

6. How did the tramp feel at the end of the meet?

_____

4 Match the words and complete them.

speed   en

west   we

beaten   er

fatter   sp

1 _____ _____ _____ _____ _____

_____ _____ _____ _____ _____

2 The words in the first column have endings.
Write the same words without endings in the second column.

_____ safely _____

_____ colder _____

_____ shortest _____

3 Write the answers to these questions:

1. How big were the tramp's meals? _____

2. Name 3 things the tramp did for work at the ranch. _____

_____

3. What did the tramp tell the rancher to do at the end of the five weeks? _____

_____

_____

4. Who wanted to bet on the tramp? _____

4 Match the words and complete them.

_____ east _____ n

_____ next _____ st

_____ meal _____ ed

_____ picked _____ m

5 Copy this sentence:
The tramp worked for five weeks.

_____

1 _____ _____ _____ _____ _____

_____ _____ _____ _____

2 The words in the first column have endings.
Write the same words without endings in the second column.

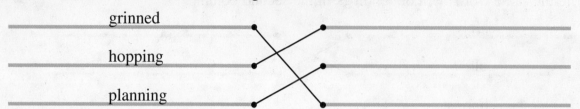

grinned

hopping

planning

3 Write the answers to these questions:

1. Where did the tramp go when there was no more work at Emma's ranch?

_____

2. What did the rancher say to the tramp just before the meet began? _____

_____

3. How much did the tramp slow down as the meet went on?

_____

4. How much did the tramp win? _____

5. Who said, "You worked so fast this week that I bet 100 dollars at five to one odds"?

_____

4 Match the words and complete them.

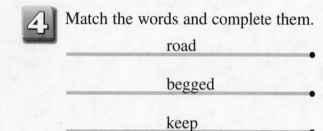

road   eep

begged   ow

keep   r

slow   ed

5 Copy this sentence:
Shelly did not get in shape.

_____

1 _____ _____ _____ _____

_____ _____ _____ _____

2 The words in the first column have endings.
Write the same words without endings in the second column.

liking _____ _____

saved _____ _____

later _____ _____

3 Look at the picture.

1. What did Rop say? "_____

_____ "

2. What did Chee say? "_____ "

4 Match the words and complete them.

luck _____ • • _____ er

shabby _____ • • _____ eeves

stacker _____ • • _____ abby

sleeves _____ • • _____ lu

1 The words in the first column have endings.
Write the same words without endings in the second column.

faster

doing

begged

named

clapped

2 Cross out the words that don't have **ea.**

sleep	neck	hear	meat	began	these
seating	smell	each	between	beat	seat

3 Write the answers to these questions:

1. What was the first thing in the meet between Rop and Chee? _____

2. What did Rop tell the worker to get? _____

_____

3. What was the score for the eating meet? _____

4. What did the workers do after Rop told his joke? _____

5. What did Chee do that made the workers ho-ho? _____

6. Where did they go for the next meet? _____

4 Match the words and complete them.

seventeen   sl

before   teen

sleeves   ed

showed   be

5 Copy this sentence:
The workers ran into the room.

_____

1 The words in the first column have endings.
Write the same words without endings in the second column.

really

cutter

making

ended

slapped

2 Cross out the words that don't have **oa.**

boat	hold	roam	float	broken	soap
short	roads	pole	goat	loading	shore

3 Write the answers to these questions:

1. What happened when Chee went very fast with the needle?

_____

2. How many sleeves did Rop slap on coats? _____

3. How many sleeves did Chee slap on coats? _____

4. What was the score for the sleeve cutting meet?

_____

5. How did Chee win the meet? _____

6. Where did Chee work after winning the meet? _____

7. Who became Chee's pal? _____

4 Match the words and complete them.

questions   be

between   sh

shame   ale

scale   ques

1 Write the words.

_____ her _____	+	_____ self _____	=	_____
_____ him _____	+	_____ self _____	=	_____
_____ your _____	+	_____ self _____	=	_____
_____ can _____	+	_____ not _____	=	_____

2 The words in the first column have endings.
Write the same words without endings in the second column.

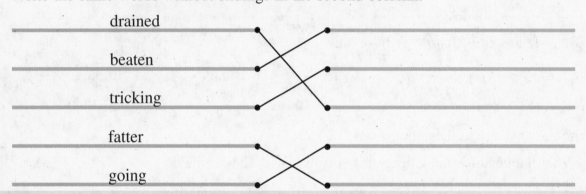

drained

beaten

tricking

fatter

going

3 Cross out the words that don't have **ee.**

hear	keep	teeth	beans	sheet	deer
three	fell	sleeps	each	between	eats

4 Write the answers to these questions:

1. Kit made a boat. What was it made of? _____

2. What did the boat do at the boat ramp? _____

3. Who told Kit not to take the boat on the lake any more? _____

   _____

4. What did Kit's boat do to the big ship at sea? _____

5. Where did Kit tell the people to swim? _____

6. What did Kit do when the water ran over the side of her boat?

   _____

5 Copy this sentence:
Her boat was a lot of fun.

_____

1 Write the words.

_____ any _____ + _____ body _____ = _____

_____ seven _____ + _____ teen _____ = _____

_____ an _____ + _____ other _____ = _____

_____ some _____ + _____ one _____ = _____

2 Cross out the words that don't have **ai.**

rain   ran   pant   paint   waited   gates

grain   may   shaved   sails   plan   fail

3 Write the answers to these questions:

1. Name the things that got into Kit's boat. _____

_____

2. What did the old woman say the goat liked to eat? _____

3. Name the things that the goat ate. _____

_____

4. How big was the hole that the goat made in the bottom of the boat?

_____

5. Who told Kit how to get back to shore? _____

4 The words in the first column have endings.
Write the same words without endings in the second column.

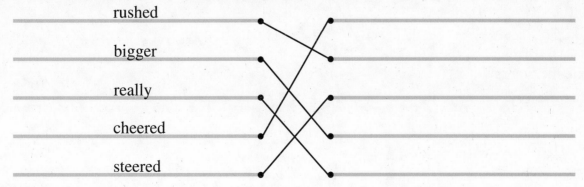

rushed

bigger

really

cheered

steered

5 Copy this sentence:
The big ship went down.

LESSON 40

1 Cross out the words that don't have **ol.**

float	gold	cold	got	shop	cold
told	broom	bolted	boat	close	old

2 Write the answers to these questions:

1. What did Kit plan to do with the big rocks?

_____

2. When the rocks are in the front of the boat, which is lower—the front or the back of the

boat? _____

3. How fast did Kit's boat go? _____

4. What fell in the boat when it went through the bank?

_____

5. What did the cop think Kit did? _____

3 The words in the first column have endings.
Write the same words without endings in the second column.

painted

leaving

ripping

closer

safely

4 Write the words.

every	+	body	=	
any	+	one	=	
some	+	body	=	
down	+	hill	=	

1 Cross out the words that don't have **oo.**

broom   cop   soon   town   kangaroo   too

who   your   moon   how   coat   room

2 Write the answers to these questions:

1. What did Kit do with the yellow paint? _____

2. Where did the boat go as it sailed through the air? _____

_____

3. How did Kit make the boat get back into the water?

_____

4. What did the fish do after it flipped its fins?

_____

5. What did Kit plan to get at the end of the story? _____

3 The words in the first column have endings.
Write the same words without endings in the second column.

making

patted

named

asked

stepped

4 Match the words and complete them.

white   ash

floating   sl

splash   wh

sleeves   cr

crunch   ing

LESSON 42

1 Cross out the words that don't have **ck.**

cat	pack	clap	clock	creek	truck
rock	neck	chops	milk	black	think

2 Write the answers to these questions:

1. Write the name of this part. _____

2. Why did the shop man have so many jobs to do? _____

_____

3. Where did Henry go for a book on motors?

_____

3 The words in the first column have endings.
Write the same words without endings in the second column.

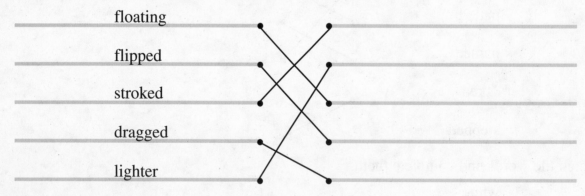

floating

flipped

stroked

dragged

lighter

4 Write the words.

_____ your + _____ self = _____

_____ up + _____ side = _____

_____ paint + _____ brush = _____

_____ any + _____ thing = _____

1 Cross out the words that don't have **wh.**

were	sweeping	where	what	woman	who
with	work	went	when	answer	which

2 Write the answers to these questions:

1. Who came in as Henry was jumping up and down? _____

2. Why was Henry yelling and jumping up and down? _____

   _____

3. Where is the pan of the motor?

   _____

4. Why did Molly have to leave?

   _____

5. What did Henry wish?

   _____

3 The words in the first column have endings.
Write the same words without endings in the second column.

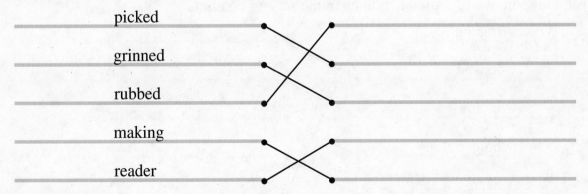

picked

grinned

rubbed

making

reader

4 Write the words.

through	+	out	=	
free	+	way	=	
with	+	out	=	
every	+	thing	=	

1 Write **1, 2,** or **3** in front of each sentence to show when these things happened in the story. Then write the sentences in the blanks.

_____ **Molly slipped into some clean clothes and ate dinner.**

_____ **Molly fixed her hot rod.**

_____ **Molly's motor broke down.**

1. _____

_____

2. _____

_____

3. _____

_____

2 Cross out the words that don't have **or.**

tore	roar	store	stroked	floating	shore
story	board	your	more	form	others

3 The words in the first column have endings.
Write the same words without endings in the second column.

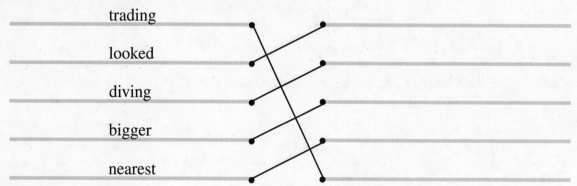

trading

looked

diving

bigger

nearest

4 Write the words.

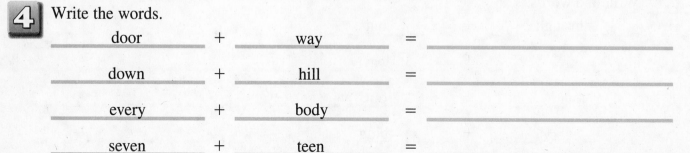

door + way =

down + hill =

every + body =

seven + teen =

1 Write **1, 2,** or **3** in front of each sentence to show when these things happened in the story. Then write the sentences in the blanks.

_____ **Kit told the con man how fast the boat went with rocks in the nose.**

_____ **Kit made a note to sell her boat.**

_____ **The con man traded five tires, his clock, his cash, and his gold ring for Kit's boat.**

1. _____

2. _____

   _____

3. _____

   _____

2 Cross out the words that don't have **ow.**

out	cow	wool	your	town	brown
how	turn	down	because	pound	order

3 The words in the first column have endings.
Write the same words without endings in the second column.

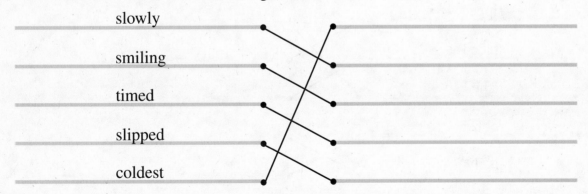

slowly

smiling

timed

slipped

coldest

4 Write the words.

in	+	side	=	_____
my	+	self	=	_____
home	+	work	=	_____
some	+	one	=	_____

1 Write the word **if.** Make a line over **f.** ——————————————

Write the word **that.** Make a line under **th.** ——————————————

2 Write **1, 2,** or **3** in front of each sentence to show when these things happened in the story. Then write the sentences in the blanks.

_____ **The con man heaped rocks into the nose of the boat.**

_____ **The boat ripped into the side of a taffy plant.**

_____ **The boat smashed into a dock and tore it to bits.**

1. ——————————————————————————

——————————————————————————

2. ——————————————————————————

——————————————————————————

3. ——————————————————————————

——————————————————————————

3 The words in the first column have endings.
Write the same words without endings in the second column.

ripped

traded

fished

robber

likely

4 Match the words and complete them.

while		ing
clear		bl
trying		ile
black		th
think		ear

1 Write the word **raining.** Make a line over **ing.** _____

Write the word **become.** Make a line under **be.** _____

2 Write the answers to these questions:

1. How did the con man look after he went through the cotton mill?

_____

2. What did the man from the dock say the con man did?

_____

3. What did the woman from the fish-packing plant say the con man did? _____

_____

4. Where did the con man tell everybody he was from?

_____

3 The words in the first column have endings.
Write the same words without endings in the second column.

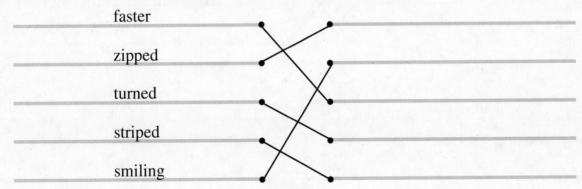

faster

zipped

turned

striped

smiling

4 Write the words.

him	+	self	=	_____
____ some ____	+	____ where ____	=	_____
____ fast ____	+	____ er ____	=	_____
____ boat ____	+	____ load ____	=	_____
____ smash ____	+	____ ing ____	=	_____

LESSON 48

1 Write the word **plant.** Make a line over **pl.** _____

Write the word **without.** Make a line under **out.** _____

2 Write the answers to these questions:

1. What did the con man do to scare the people? _____

_____

2. What did the cops do when the con man scared them?

_____

3. What did the con man take from the bank?

_____

4. What did the con man slip on after he left the bank?

_____

3 The words in the first column have endings.
Write the same words without endings in the second column.

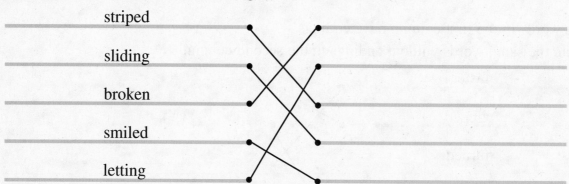

striped

sliding

broken

smiled

letting

4 Write the words.

some	+	thing	=	
through	+	out	=	
fast	+	est	=	
up	+	side	=	
every	+	thing	=	

5 Copy this sentence:
The cotton lint was sticking to taffy.

1 Write the word **someone.** Make a line over **one.** _____

Write the word **licked.** Make a line under **ed.** _____

2 Write **1, 2,** or **3** in front of each sentence to show when these things happened in the story. Then write the sentences in the blanks.

_____ **The con man told the jailer that he was sick.**

_____ **The cops and nine dogs led the con man to the jail.**

_____ **Cats, dogs, and goats began licking taffy.**

1. _____

_____

2. _____

_____

3. _____

_____

3 The words in the first column have endings.
Write the same words without endings in the second column.

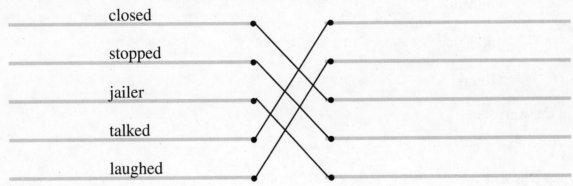

closed

stopped

jailer

talked

laughed

4 Write the words.

late	+	er	=	_____
paint	+	brush	=	_____
door	+	way	=	_____
in	+	side	=	_____
home	+	work	=	_____

LESSON 50

1 Write the word **hotter.** Make a line over **hot.** _____

Write the word **scream.** Make a line under **ea.** _____

2 Write the answers to these questions:

1. Why did the digging bug dig?

_____

2. When it got hot, where did the other bugs go?

_____

3. What did the dusty bug tell the other bugs to give him?

_____

4. What did the mother bug give the dusty bug?

_____

3 The words in the first column have endings.
Write the same words without endings in the second column.

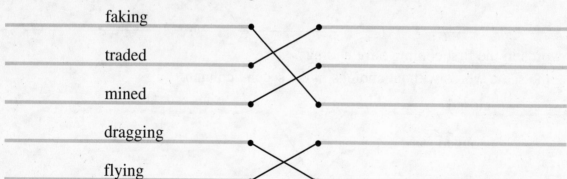

faking _____

traded _____

mined _____

dragging _____

flying _____

4 Write the words.

free	+	way	=	
sleep	+	ing	=	
with	+	out	=	
my	+	self	=	
be	+	come	=	

5 Copy this sentence:
The bugs went inside the hole.

_____

1 Write the word **these**. Make a line over **th**. _____

Write the word **outside**. Make a line under **side**. _____

2 Write **1, 2,** or **3** in front of each sentence to show when these things happened in the story. Then write the sentences in the blanks.

_____ The dusty bug burped and went back to his mine.

_____ The bug went to a store.

_____ The bug dug into the tub and got a big dill.

1. _____

_____

2. _____

_____

3. _____

_____

3 The words in the first column have endings.
Write the same words without endings in the second column.

riding

shapely

rested

smoking

patted

4 Match the words and complete them.

space   dr

must   ee

stayed   sp

drain   mu

three   ed

LESSON 52

1 Write the word **clock.** Make a line over **ck.** _____

Write the word **grabbed.** Make a line under **grab.** _____

2 Write the answers to these questions:

1. What did the old clock maker like to do when he wasn't working on clocks?

_____

2. When the clock works, what comes out every hour? _____

3. How much was the clock maker's bid for fixing the clock? _____

3 The words in the first column have endings.
Write the same words without endings in the second column.

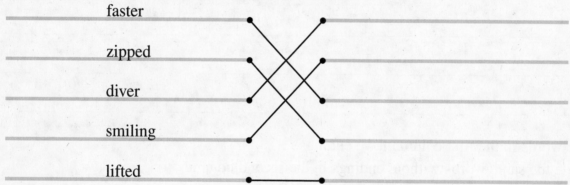

faster

zipped

diver

smiling

lifted

4 Write the words.

her	+	self	=	
can	+	not	=	
down	+	hill	=	
land	+	ing	=	
boat	+	load	=	

5 Copy this sentence:
The old clock maker did not hear her.

_____

1 Write the word **dropping.** Make a line over **drop.** _____

Write the word **deer.** Make a line under **ee.** _____

2 Write **1, 2,** or **3** in front of each sentence to show when these things happened in the story. Then write the answers in the blanks.

_____ **The deer bobbed up and down like a frog.**

_____ **The woman tossed the clock down.**

_____ **The clock maker painted the clock orange.**

1. _____

_____

2. _____

_____

3. _____

_____

3 The words in the first column have endings.
Write the same words without endings in the second column.

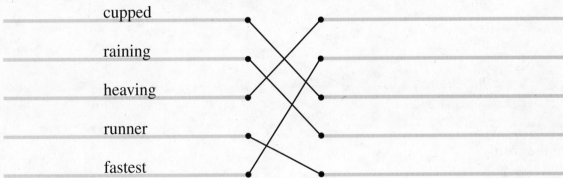

cupped

raining

heaving

runner

fastest

4 Write the words.

every + body = _____

up + side = _____

heat + er = _____

every + thing = _____

home + work = _____

Write the word **suddenly.** Make a line over **ly.** _____

Write the word **painted.** Make a line under **ed.** _____

 Write the answers to these questions:

1. The clock maker's wife told him that a little girl wanted to do something.

What was that? _____

2. How much did the wife plan to pay the girl if she did a good job?

_____

3. How did the clock maker hide the dent in the side of the clock?

_____

4. What did the alligator do to the clock maker? _____

5. How did the clock maker make the alligator look like a deer?_____

_____

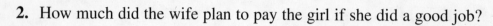 The words in the first column have endings.
Write the same words without endings in the second column.

joking	
smiled	
maker	
holding	
dropped	

 Write the words.

your	+	self	=	
some	+	one	=	
any	+	body	=	
paint	+	brush	=	
through	+	out	=	

1. What did the woman say? " _____

_____ "

2. What did the clock maker say? " _____

_____ "

The words in the first column have endings.
Write the same words without endings in the second column.

slapped

taking

looked

wiped

sounded

Write the words.

door	+	way	=	
be	+	come	=	
with	+	out	=	
loud	+	ly	=	
in	+	side	=	

Copy this sentence:
The clock maker rapped on her door.

1 Write the name of the person each sentence tells about.

        con man   **doctor**

1. This person barked like a dog.

    _____

2. This person worked at the rest home.

    _____

3. This person took notes on a pad.

    _____

4. This person said, "Have you ever felt
   like anything else—a goat, or a farmer?"

    _____

5. This person said, "I am the king fox."

    _____

2 Write the answer to this question:

Why did the nurse at the hospital think that the con man had gone mad?

_____

3 The words in the first column have endings.
Write the same words without endings in the second column.

stared	
fastest	
runner	
stepping	
loudly	

4 Match the words and complete them.

farmer	doc
thank	er
because	etty
doctor	th
pretty	be

5 Write the 1st sentence of Story 56.

_____

_____

Write the name of the person each sentence tells about.
    con man   **president**

1. This person said, "I am the father of our country." _____

2. This person came up with a fine plan to escape
   from the room. _____

3. This person said, "I will do whatever you say." _____

4. This person did not want to be a private. _____

5. This person gave orders. _____

The words in the first column have endings.
Write the same words without endings in the second column.

_____ talking _____
_____ fired _____
_____ kidding _____
_____ really _____
_____ maker _____

Write the words.

_____ out _____ + _____ side _____ = _____

_____ any _____ + _____ thing _____ = _____

_____ may _____ + _____ be _____ = _____

_____ what _____ + _____ ever _____ = _____

_____ farm _____ + _____ er _____ = _____

Write the 2nd sentence of Story 57.

_____

_____

1 Write the name of the person each sentence tells about.

con man   **president**

1. This person took lots of orders.   _____

2. Dust makes this person sneeze.   _____

3. This person kept a sharp look out for the helpers.   _____

4. This person ate three plates of wheat cakes.   _____

5. This person hid in the grove of trees.   _____

6. This person screamed that his foot was
stuck in the gate.   _____

2 The words in the first column have endings.
Write the same words without endings in the second column.

firing   _____

hotter   _____

talked   _____

wiped   _____

washing   _____

3 Write the word **coach.** Make a line over **oa.** _____

Write the word **without.** Make a line under **out.** _____

4 Write the 3rd sentence of Story 58.

_____

_____

1 Write the answers to these questions:

1. How many people ran after the con man and the president? _____

2. Why did the president say he needed a car? _____

_____

3. Which car did the woman let the con man and the president take?

_____

4. Where did the con man and the president stop to rest? _____

5. What did the president say to the man at the front desk?_____

_____

_____

6. Why didn't the man at the desk want the president to talk in a loud voice?

_____

2 The words in the first column have endings.
Write the same words without endings in the second column.

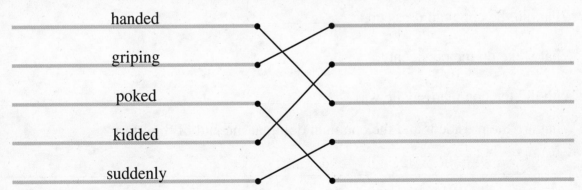

handed

griping

poked

kidded

suddenly

3 Match the words and complete them.

should   ust

remember   wh

yard   sh

crust   ard

wheat   re

1 Write **1, 2,** or **3** in front of each sentence to show when these things happened in the story. Then write the sentences in the blanks.

_____ **The con man put on a bridal dress.**

_____ **The president ordered the con man to charge a big lunch to the bridal room.**

_____ **The president told the con man that his hair was very pretty.**

1. _____

_____

2. _____

_____

3. _____

_____

2 Write the answers to these questions:

1. What did the con man dress up as? _____

2. What woke up the president? _____

3. Who did the con man say he was? _____

4. What are the president and the con man doing at the end of this story?

_____

3 The words in the first column have endings.
Write the same words without endings in the second column.

digging

handing

griped

broken

washed

Write the name of the person each sentence tells about.

man at the desk   con man   president

1. This person was dressed up like a bride.   _____

2. This person stuck a beard on his chin.   _____

3. This person said there were bugs in the bridal room.   _____

4. This person said, "Don't say anything about bugs."   _____

5. This person wanted two hundred dollars.   _____

6. This person was conned out of two hundred dollars.   _____

2 Write the words.

_____with_____ + _____out_____ = _____

_____no_____ + _____body_____ = _____

_____near_____ + _____by_____ = _____

_____any_____ + _____one_____ = _____

_____near_____ + _____est_____ = _____

3 Match the words and complete them.

lunch • • sh

would • • ch

darted • • ing

shirt • • w

outing • • ed

 Write the 1st sentence of Story 61.

_____

_____

LESSON 62

1 Write the answers to these questions:

1. Why didn't anybody like night patrol?

   _____

2. Where did the drams live? _____

3. What did drams look like? _____

   _____

4. What happened about three times a year? _____

   _____

5. How long had Jean been on the planet?

   _____

6. As Jean was on patrol, she kept thinking about the drams. What was one of the questions

   she asked herself? _____

   _____

   _____

2 The words in the first column have endings.
Write the same words without endings in the second column.

raining

liked

helper

grinned

eaten

3 Write the word **eating.** Make a line over **eat.** _____

Write the word **first.** Make a line under **ir.** _____

1 Write the name of the person each sentence tells about.

Jean   major   Carla

1. This person was frozen as she looked at the drams. _____

2. This person signaled the barracks that the drams were coming. _____

3. This person said to take it easy. _____

4. This person was not with all the other women. _____

5. This person went back to the barracks. _____

6. This person had a trumpet next to her bed. _____

7. This person was in the barracks when parts of the wall fell down. _____

2 The words in the first column have endings.
Write the same words without endings in the second column.

suddenly

smiled

taking

pounded

snapping

3 Write the words.

bright	+	ness	=	
every	+	thing	=	
day	+	time	=	
any	+	body	=	
moon	+	light	=	

4 Write the 2nd sentence of Story 63.

_____

_____

1 Write **1, 2,** or **3** in front of each sentence to show the order that these things happened in the story.

_____ **Jean grabbed the trumpet and started to blow it.**

_____ **The drams bit Jean.**

_____ **The drams went to sleep.**

2 Write the answers to these questions:

1. When Jean ran from Carla's room, what were the drams doing?

_____

2. Jean fell into a hole in the barracks. How did that hole get there?

_____

3. What did the women do to help Jean?

_____

4. Why didn't Jean find Carla in the barracks? _____

_____

5. Why did the major say that she would have to report Jean?

_____

6. What did Jean do that was brave? _____

3 The words in the first column have endings.
Write the same words without endings in the second column.

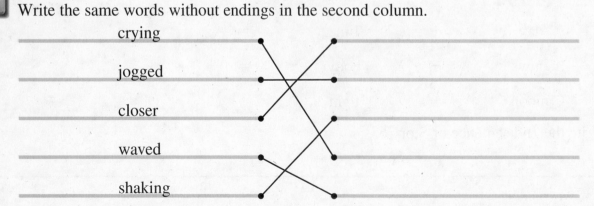

crying

jogged

closer

waved

shaking

1 Write the name of the person each sentence tells about.
      Jean   **major**

1. This person gave a blast on the trumpet.

   _____

2. This person told the women why the trumpet made the drams sleep.

   _____

3. This person said that the women can pipe sound into the lake.

   _____

4. This person felt very proud because she showed the women how to stop the drams.

   _____

2 Match the words and complete them.

trying •   • es

frozen •   • inked

escaped •   • fr

shouted •   • ing

blinked •   • sh

3 Write the words.

spot + light = _____

some + thing = _____

no + body = _____

out + side = _____

her + self = _____

4 Write the word **always.** Make a line over **al.** _____

Write the word **sight.** Make a line under **igh.** _____

5 Write the 3rd sentence of Story 65.

_____

_____

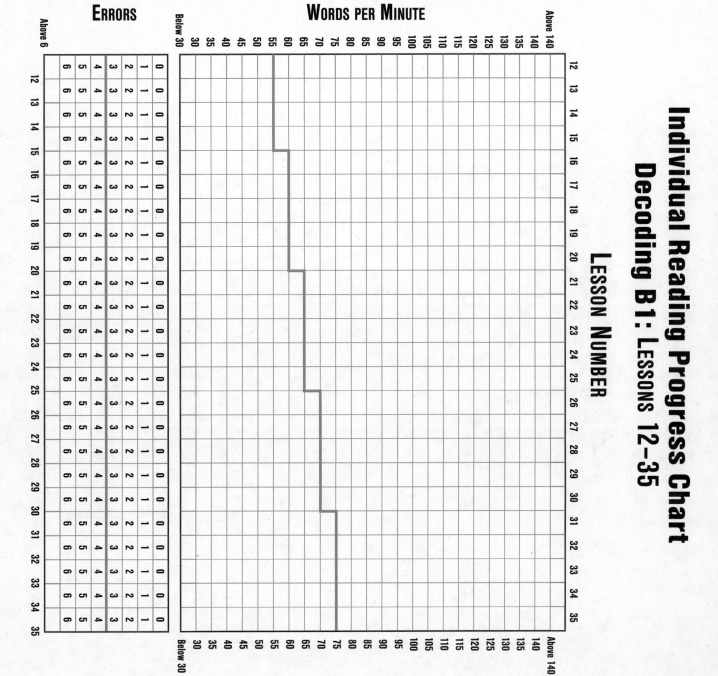

Individual Reading Progress Chart

Decoding B1: Lessons 12–35

ERRORS

WORDS PER MINUTE

LESSON NUMBER

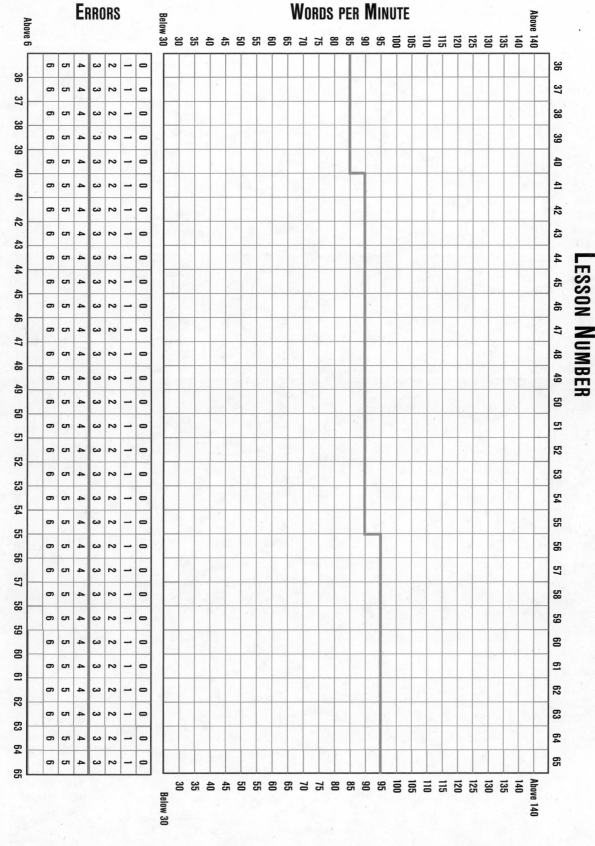

Individual Reading Progress Chart
Decoding B1: Lessons 36-65

ERRORS

WORDS PER MINUTE

LESSON NUMBER